Acknowledgements

Educational consultant Viv Edwards, Professor of
Language in Education, University of Reading.
Illustrations by Steve Cox.
Photographs by Zul Mukhida except for:
pp.4t, 6t John Heinrich, 8, 9t, 14b Tim Garrod, back cover (left) Doug Green,
Zul Colour Library; p.14t Newport Photographic; p.15 Food Features;
p.16t Andes Press Agency; p.16b Sally Fear; p.17 Prodeepta Das.

The author and publisher would like to thank: the staff and
pupils of Balfour Infant School, Brighton and Somerhill
Junior School, Hove; Simon Hart; Marks & Spencer plc;
Asda Group plc; H.J. Heinz Co. Ltd; Cheungs Chinese Restaurant

A CIP catalogue record for this book is available
from the British Library.

ISBN 0-7136-4029-4

First published 1994 by A & C Black (Publishers) Ltd
35 Bedford Row, London WC1R 4JH

© 1994 A & C Black (Publishers) Ltd

Typeset in 15/21pt Univers Medium by
Rowland Phototypesetting Ltd, Bury St Edmunds, Suffolk.
Printed in Belgium by Proost International Book Production.

Food

Nicola Edwards

A & C Black · London

Some kinds of food
have messages
on them.

How many different
messages can you
see on the food in
this picture? What
do the messages
tell you?

Food is often sold in packages, such as bags, boxes and tubs. These packages have messages on them which tell you about the food inside.

The tin on the right has lost its label. The girl will have to open the tin to find out what sort of food is inside it.

The label on the boy's tin tells him:

the name of the food inside the tin

that it does not contain meat

how to heat up the soup

the name of the company that made the soup

the different foods, or ingredients, in the soup

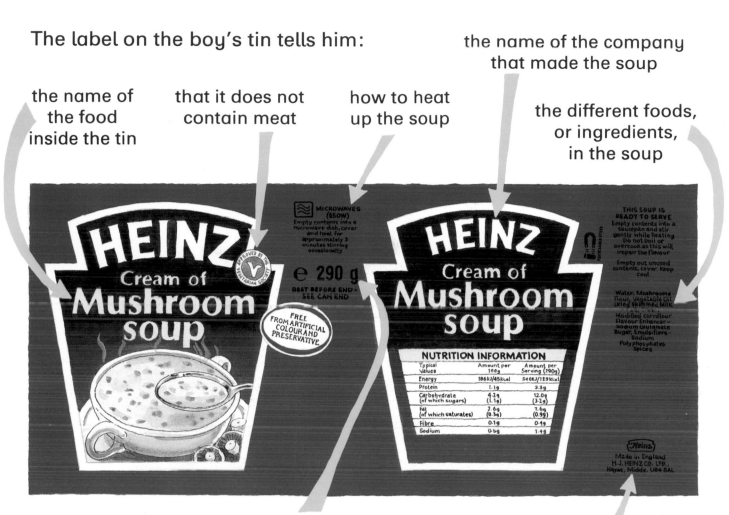

how much the soup inside the tin weighs

the country where the soup was made

Have a look at some packages of food in your kitchen at home. How many different messages can you find about the food which is inside each package?

People use messages
to sell food.

The signs on this market
stall show the prices of
the fruit and vegetables.

The signs in this
supermarket tell you
where you can find
each kind of food.

The labels on the shelves tell you how much each package of food weighs and how much it costs.

The signs at this delicatessen counter show the prices of the different foods.

The sign on the outside of this building tells you that it is a restaurant where you can buy something to eat.

Some restaurants have a menu outside. A menu is a list of the different meals you can choose from, and their prices.

Some restaurants have pictures showing the different meals you can choose from.

Are there any restaurants near your home? How do they tell you about the food they serve?

Inside a restaurant you can look at a menu to help you decide what food to order.

What food would you choose from this menu?
How much does it cost?

MENU

LUNCH

MAIN COURSE

Roast Beef and Yorkshire Pudding ... £4·00
Shepherd's Pie ... £3·50
Vegetable Lasagne ... £3·75
Cheese and Tomato Pizza ... £3·00
Cauliflower Cheese ... £2·75
Sausage, Beans and Chips ... £3·25

DESSERT

Trifle ... £2·00
Chocolate Sponge and Custard ... £2·25
Apple Pie and Cream ... £2·50
Fruit Salad ... £1·75
Ice Cream ... £1·50
(Vanilla, Chocolate, Raspberry Ripple)

In some restaurants you tell a waiter what food you would like.
This waitress is writing down the order to take to the kitchen.

At the end of the meal the waiter gives you a bill which tells you how much you have to pay.

DRAGON RESTAURANT
45 CANTON ROW · SOHO · LONDON W1

Table 5

Prawn Crackers	£ 0.75
Vegetable Spring Roll	£ 1.50
Chicken Chow Mein	£ 3.00
Egg Fried Rice	£ 1.50
Sweet and Sour Pork	£ 3.25
Boiled Rice	£ 1.00
King Prawns	£ 3.50
Noodles	£ 2.00
Mineral Water	£ 0.75
Lemonade	£ 0.75

TOTAL £ 18.00

When people cook at home, they often follow a recipe which tells them what to do.

The boy in these pictures is following a recipe to help him make some fairy cakes.

First he mixes the sugar and butter and adds the beaten egg.

Fairy cakes

100g butter
100g castor sugar
2 beaten eggs
150g self-raising flour
50g currants

Next the recipe tells him to mix in the flour and currants.

Then he spoons the cake mixture into paper cases.

His mum puts the cakes into the oven. After 15 minutes the cakes are ready. They taste delicious!

Sometimes food can show that people are celebrating a special occasion, such as a wedding.

Children have brought this food to their local temple to celebrate a harvest festival.

Which special occasion do you think
the food in this picture is celebrating?

What's your favourite party food?

Food is an important part of many religious festivals.

In this Christian ceremony, people are given a wafer to remind them of the body of Jesus Christ.

This food has been specially prepared to celebrate the Jewish festival of Passover.

During the Hindu festival of Diwali, people bring food to the temple to offer to the gods.

Some kinds of food can make you think of different times of the day.

At what time of day would you eat each of these meals?

Some foods can tell you when they're ready to eat. They can also warn you not to eat them.

Which of these tomatoes would you eat? Why?

Have you ever tried to describe the
taste of a food?

See if you can collect the four different
foods in this picture. Which words
would you use to describe how they taste?

Ask some friends to taste the foods.
How do they describe the different tastes?

For parents and teachers

The aim of the *Messages* series is to help build confidence in children who are just beginning to read by encouraging them to make meaning from the different kinds of signs and symbols which surround them in their everyday lives. Here are some suggestions for follow-up activities which extend the ideas introduced in the book.

Pages 2/3 Set up a classroom display to show the variety of messages found on items of food. Include food from different cultures with messages other than English. The children could make some food out of modelling clay and put their own made-up messages on it.

Pages 4/5 Make a collection of food packaging as a starting point for a variety of activities. How far has the food travelled from where it was originally grown or made? On a world map, pin the name of each food to its country of origin and use wool to show the distance travelled to Britain. Make a list of the food produced by each country. You could also talk about how different kinds of food are processed and preserved. The children could bring in examples of dried, pickled, tinned and frozen foods to compare with the foods in their raw state.

Pages 6/7 Use empty food boxes and food made out of modelling clay to set up a market stall in the classroom. The children could make price labels and signs describing the different food and posters advertising special offers.

Pages 8/9 Make a classroom menu, listing the children's favourite meals and their made-up prices. Add pictures drawn by the children or cut out of magazines to illustrate the menu. Many take-away restaurants give away menus which you could use to show the children the different ways in which meals are described.

Pages 10/11 Using the classroom menu from the previous activity, the children can take turns to be a customer and a waiter ordering a meal and noting down the order. The children could also try making up their own coded shorthand in which to take down the order.

Pages 12/13 Collect the ingredients for a simple recipe which can be prepared in the classroom and cooked in the school kitchen. The children can take it in turns to weigh out the ingredients and mix them together. What changes do the children notice in the look, smell and feel of the food, before and after it is cooked?

Pages 14/15 Find out about the origins and importance of food in the celebration of different festivals around the world. In the United States, for example, pumpkins, sweet potatoes and turkey are eaten on Thanksgiving Day. During the Chinese New Year, foods take on a symbolic significance with, for instance, peanuts, melon seeds and preserved fruits traditionally representing prosperity, longevity and happiness, and sticky cakes made with glutinous rice symbolising family unity. The children may have photographs of their family celebrating a special occasion (such as a wedding or Christmas Day) which could be used to decorate a classroom display.

Pages 16/17 Find out about the symbolic importance of food in different religions, using the children's own experience as a starting point. Are any of the children vegetarian as part of their religion? Find out about the origins of such symbols as the unleavened bread eaten during the Jewish Passover, the honey-dipped apples eaten as part of the Jewish celebrations for Rosh Hashanah, the pancakes traditionally made on Shrove Tuesday, the hot-cross buns eaten on Good Friday and the chocolate eggs given as presents on Easter Sunday.

Pages 18/19 Make a list of the foods the children associate with different times of the day. The children could carry out a survey to find out about the range of foods eaten at different meal times. What do the children think is a healthy menu for the day?

Pages 20/21 Show the children examples of fruit and vegetables in varying degrees of ripeness. How does the change in colour, texture and taste of a food signal that it is ready to eat? Experiment with different ways of keeping food fresh. For example, store one slice of bread in an air-tight box, one in a plastic bag in a fridge and one in the open air. What signals do the children notice which tell them that the bread is no longer fresh?

Pages 22/23 Give the children examples of different foods and ask them to describe the taste. Divide the foods into different categories (eg. salty, bitter, sweet, sour and others mentioned by the children) and display the findings on a wallchart.